H

is for

Healing

Magick

Kitchen Table Magick Series

by

G. Alan Joel

ISBN-13: 979-8-9856257-3-8

Email: **_alan@shamanschool.com_**
Website: **_www.shamanschool.com_**

Publisher: Esoteric School of Shamanism and Magic, Inc.

Disclaimer and Legal Notice:
The Esoteric School of Shamanism and Magic has made every effort to ensure, at the time of this writing, that the information contained in this book is as accurate as possible. The publisher and author make no warranties or representation with respect to the completeness, fitness, accuracy, applicability, or appropriateness of this book's contents. This book's information is provided strictly for entertainment and educational purposes. Should you choose to use or apply the ideas provided in this book, you take full responsibility for your own actions. The publisher and author provide no guarantee that your life will improve in any way should you choose to use the information presented in this book. The ability of the information provided in this book to provide self-help and life improvement to the reader is entirely dependent upon the reader. The reader's ability to gain positive results from the information presented in this book is entirely dependent on the amount of time the reader devotes to the application of the material in this book, the willingness of the reader to dedicate time and effort to learning the materials presented in this book, as well as the reader's own belief system, which may help or hinder the reader's ability to benefit from this book's materials. Since each reader differs according to willingness and openness to the information available in this book, the author and publisher cannot guarantee success or improvement for every individual reader. Neither the publisher nor the author assumes responsibility for the reader's actions, or whether the information is used for negative or positive purposes. The information contained in this book is drawn from tribal traditions—both modern and ancient—as well as the author's 30 plus years' experience researching and teaching this material to students. The information in this book is presented as interpreted by the author, and, as such, may or may not be entirely accurate. In no way should the information presented in this book be a substitute for advice from health or mental health professionals. The author and publisher are not liable—or in any way responsible—for actions

that the reader may or may not take as a result of reading the information contained in this book. The reader assumes full responsibility for his or her own actions and choices with regard to how he or she chooses to use the information in this book. The reader is strongly encouraged to choose to use the information provided in this book responsibly.

[this page intentionally left blank]

Healing Magick Blessing

Child of Wonder,
Child of Flame
Nourish Our Spirits and
Protect Our Aim.

My personal space be filled with Magick and healing,
I summon positive energies that are within me indwelling!
Angels, Totems, and Healing Spirits abound,
I call ye forth, your healing energies about me surround!

Negative energies in the "real world" be disconnected,
Through simple and powerful rituals, intentionally directed!
The pendulum swung with focus and love,
Unwinds discomfort and pain, with help from above!

Electric blue spirals I see whirling and strong,
Burning up within me anything negative or wrong!
Higher powers I greet with the Beauty Way ritual,
Their assistance for healing be both physical and spiritual!

Directing my energies with purpose and no doubt,
I push through blockages so no illnesses may sprout!
Air, Fire, Water and Earth,
These four elements have true healing worth!

Thus, my will, so mote it be!

Free Gift

To thank you for purchasing this book, I'd like to give you a

100% FREE GIFT

Learn more about your free magickal gift.

Access Your Free Gift at
www.shamanschool.com

Find a complete list of magickal resources on https://amzn.to/3swxvP0. These resources are constantly updated so check back often!

[this page intentionally left blank]

Kitchen Table Healing Magick
Table of Contents

[this page intentionally left blank]

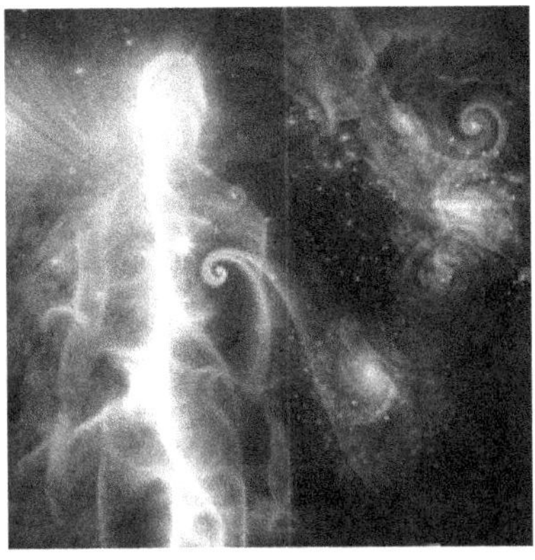

Introduction to Kitchen Table Healing Magick

"We're asking you to trust in the Well-being. In optimism there is magic."
~Abraham

A Note About This Introduction

This book is one of a series of books in the Kitchen Table Magick series. Each book in the series addresses a specific area of magick (love, money, psychic development, etc.), and is written in a simple "recipe" format for people who want to use magick in their lives immediately. The Kitchen Table Magick series is akin to a Julia Childs recipe book, only these books contain magickal recipes for people to cook up some miraculous and magickal manifestations in their lives.

Because this series was designed so that each person could pick and choose to read just the books that pertain to their current life situation, each book is meant to be readable as a stand-alone book. To introduce the new reader to the series, this introduction to the series is repeated at the beginning of each book. If you have already read one or more books in this series, please feel free to jump ahead to the recipes that interest you. At the same time, some people feel that reviewing the introduction, as well as the "Rules and Tips," is helpful before diving in. In magickal circles, your will is the guideline so choose whichever route best suits you… the Universe and magickal beings will follow!

What is Magick?

Many people have multiple different ideas about what magick is or can be. For the sake of clarity, here is what we know about magick after more than 35 years of study and practice. Magick is a precision science! It is also:

- The science of deliberate creation.
- The science of effective prayer.
- The science of manifesting Higher Will (substitute whatever Higher Force is most familiar to you) on the energetic and material planes.
- The science of heightened awareness, selective perception, and dynamic, harmonious relationships.
- The study of intention (as per Aleister Crowley, one of the greatest magickal practitioners in history).
- The system of creation, not coercion. Note: The word manipulation is often used in conjunction with magick, but manipulation simply means the use of the hands. It should be an "OK" word without a lot of charge, but currently it is used mostly to mean coercion. Look it up!
- The principle that every intentional act is a magickal act! Magic gives us the ability to communicate with beings on all levels, and allows us to understand, through direct experience, the actual workings of the Universe.
- The traditional path of spiritual growth.
- Not extraordinary knowledge. It is the "normal" way of life. We've just lost access to it. When you have this kind of knowledge in your understanding, you have the ability to resolve spiritual questions that otherwise become catechism. From a magickal point of view, catechism is not acceptable, since a practitioner must experience and verify everything for him or herself. It

avoids the trap of dogma. In past times, having a magickal foundation was essential so that we could talk directly to higher beings in the Universal hierarchy.

- Necessary to effective religious practice.

There is some confusion as to how to spell the word "magick." There are three different commonly used spellings: magick, magic, and majick. Eliphas Levi first used the form "magick" to differentiate religious or ceremonial from stage magick. All forms of spelling are acceptable in what this author teaches.

"The Kitchen Table Magick book series is practical, simple, effective, and, best of all, requires almost no special ingredients. This rituals in this book series can definitely be done at your kitchen table!"
~Whitney L., Rapid City, SD

Is Magick Real?

Yes. Magick is very real and has existed as a precise science for thousands of years. Whether you use the word magick or another name, this spiritual practice is very real. Every single person can learn to do magick. We are ALL born with the talents and abilities that empower us to do magick. The only reason that magick seems so, well, magickal is that this society no longer teaches the art and science of magick. In the distant past, magickal study was just as important as math, science, or the arts. In fact, magick was and still is the birthright of EVERY planetary citizen.

Can you learn to do the kind of magick portrayed in the movies? Yes... and no. The movies are great at giving you a taste of what you can do with magick, but they are not very accurate. In the Harry Potter movies, for instance, the characters use their Wands for every magickal operation. In reality, you can only use the Wand to handle Air energies. Your Wand would actually explode or catch fire if you tried to use it to throw Firebolts and Fireballs as the characters do in the movie.

So, what can you actually do with magick? Quite a lot. Here is a short list to get you started:

- Balance your energies for healing and manifestation
- Change old beliefs
- Defend yourself against physical and psychic attack
- Heal yourself and others
- Find hidden information and see possible futures (and change the future if you do not like the probable futures you divine)
- Psychically communicate with other beings
- Create sacred space
- Find lost people and objects
- Manifest what you want and need in life

At the very basis of magick is the understanding of the four elements: Air, Fire, Water, and Earth. Called elemental magick, these foundational elements are real. Air, Fire, Water and Earth are part of our natural everyday environment. What makes them magickal is the understanding of how they operate not just on the physical level, but also at the levels of Mind and Spirit.

For instance, while on the physical level, Air is just the stuff we breathe. On the magickal levels Air is the conduit of psychic communication, enlightenment, understanding, dreaming, and more. If you want more of these things in your life, then you need more magickal Air. How do you get more magickal Air? Wear more Air colors, including white for communication and sky blue for enlightenment and understanding. To take this one step further, you could also use various magickal techniques to take on more Air to make your body lighter. Take on enough Air and you'll be able to levitate.

By just extending your understanding and use of the basic ingredients of nature, you are doing magick! Seen in this light, magick isn't all smoke and mirrors, nor is it the result of Hollywood special effects. Magic is the result of truly understanding and working with the very elements that are all around you.

One final note: Many masters, including Wayne Dyer, have said, "You'll see it when you believe it." The same is true for magick. In other words, the suspension of disbelief and the willingness not to exercise contempt prior to investigation are requirements for magick to be "real." Magick is all around us, and always is, but our ability to perceive and use the forces of magick depends on our willingness to be open. No one else can show it to you, only your direct experience and observation can "prove" or demonstrate to you that magick is real.

What is Kitchen Table Magick?

Kitchen Table Magick is exactly what it sounds like—a series of simple recipes that you can literally "cook up" at your kitchen table using household ingredients from your own pantry and cupboard.

The Kitchen Table Magic books have been created for ordinary people who want to mix up a little magick in their lives without all the fancy rituals, but simply with everyday ingredients that can be found in the kitchen pantry, bathroom medicine cabinet, or even stuffed in the back of the junk drawer.

The goal of these books is to allow anyone with the desire to learn this craft to mix up magick literally at the kitchen table using simple recipes. What goes into a simple recipe?

- Everyday items as ingredients
- Easy to follow instructions that don't require years of training
- Procedures that take less than two hours from start to finish
- Built-in expertise that allows the magick to do the heavy lifting
- Some friendly advice on how you can help your magickal recipe provide the best results
- Oh, and a few little rules and guidelines about magickal practice in this specific arena that will keep you safe and sound, magickally speaking, when you use these recipes

Kitchen Table Magick Equals:
Quick – Effective – Safe – Everyday Use – Ordinary
Affordable Ingredients

Why Use Kitchen Table Magic?

- Everyone can do magick.
- Magick should be simple, effective, and start working right away, else it is not magick.
- Not everyone has the time or resources to enroll in a school.
- People ask us for magickal help in hundreds of emails everyday... Kitchen Table Magick is designed to help these very people.
- Of the many areas of life, most people only seem to need help in one or two areas, so you need only buy those Kitchen Table Magick books that apply to your needs.
- Magic is for the masses, and should be accessible, affordable, and simple to do. This is what our teacher taught us, and this is the legacy we are paying forward as well.
- While there are many more advanced forms of magick, these books are an introduction to that world so that you can dabble, experiment, try things out, see the result, adjust and amend, and generally have fun... just as you would cooking a meal in your kitchen.
- This book is not for the major foodie, but is perfect for the person who needs magickal help right here, right now!

Who Should Use These Recipes?

- You and anyone you know who would like a little more magick and a little less ordinary reality in their lives
- Anyone who needs help RIGHT now and doesn't have time to fly to India or Sedona to sit at the feet of a guru

- Anyone who does not have access to anything but a computer for help and guidance
- Anyone who wants to do magick and then forget it (all while quietly watching the magick "do its thing")
- Anyone who wants affordable, down to earth magick they can do with regular ingredients in the comfort of home

When to Use Kitchen Table Magic: Anytime...

- You need help
- You don't want to do all the heavy lifting (leave that to the angels, Spirit guides, animal totems, and so forth)
- You seem stuck in a rut or corner with no way out
- You've been struggling with a problem for a long time and need a resolution
- You don't know what to do but you need to do SOMETHING
- You'd like to learn how to practice the craft
- You want to live a more magickal life and stop dealing with ordinary hassles all the time

How Do We Know These Recipes Work?

- We teach a slew of these recipes in one-day workshops all over the country, via teleconference, and via videoconference. We also email them to people as part of our school's service work, or post them on our blogs and articles library.
- We have used them for over 35 years and still do, every single day – literally tested out at our own kitchen tables for over 35 years, and at thousands of kitchen tables around the world for a quarter century or more
- We receive all kinds of stories and testimonials from happy successful students.

Kitchen Table Healing Magick at Work...

Read the following examples to discover how Healing Magick works in real life...

Magickally Unwinding a Twisted Ankle

I have always believed in magick in a casual way because I grew up around it. My parents were "Earth Religionists," which meant that they believed that healing powers could be found in Earth, Sun, Sky, Water, and Nature. I participated in some of their "magickal" rituals when I was a child, but I never really focused on the purpose or results of the rituals.

As an adult, I moved away from my hometown and my parents. I promptly forgot almost all of the rituals I had learned during my early years, and was completely immersed in my career, my own children, and all the details of everyday life. My children and I are all athletic, and participated in a number of sports—from tennis and soccer to hockey and football.

It wasn't until I twisted my ankle badly in soccer practice, just a few days before a big playoff match, that I was reminded of some of the healing rituals that I had learned from my parents.

I was complaining to my mom about my ankle (and how I would probably have to sit on the sidelines during the playoffs) when my mom asked me if I had tried healing my ankle using magick. I told her that I could not remember the rituals, and that the playoff game was only a few days away; there was no way my ankle would heal fast enough for me to participate in the playoffs.

My mom just laughed (and bet me that magick could heal my ankle fast enough for me the join the next playoff match). She quickly reviewed some of the simple rituals for healing; she reminded me how to use a pendulum to unwind my twisted ankle, push energy boxes through my ankle to clear stuck energies, and create an electric blue spiral to burn through any inflammation.

Because I really wanted to take part in the playoffs, I followed her instructions to the letter. I used all three rituals several times daily before the playoffs. As you might guess, I lost the bet! But I was delighted to pay my mother for the lost bet (I sent her a batch of my special homemade cookies, which she adored),

Being able to take part in the playoff games was worth it! I would have cooked my mother a five-course meal if I could send it through the mail. But cookies were more than enough for my mom. She was

delighted that I had returned to my magickal roots, and I was thrilled that I could play soccer with a magickally-healed ankle!
~ Louise P., Valley City, ND

[this page intentionally left blank]

A Few Rules and Tips About Kitchen Table Magick

As with any game, the game of life has its own set of rules. Specifically, the spiritual side of life has rules. Play by those rules and you will stay safe and easily attract what you want into your life. Break those rules and all types of unwanted consequences happen.

These "spiritual rules" are ones that have been observed, both in personal spiritual practice and spiritual practice with various associated groups and teachers. These rules universally govern any spiritual practice, and appear to be in effect whether you know them or not. Unlike ethics and morals, which change with culture and time, these spiritual rules appear to have remained the same throughout time, unchanging, like physical and scientific rules.

The rules in the following section are adapted from *Rules of the Road*, as created by George Dew, co-founder of the Church of Seven Arrows. There are two major rules, which are common to most spiritual practices, along with some minor rules that are specific to our form of magickal practice.

Two Major Rules

These two rules will probably sound familiar, as they appear in most major religions and spiritual practices, most probably because they are common-sense and apply not just to spiritual practice, but to life as well.

First Rule: Golden Rule or Law of Karma
This first rule is literally a "golden oldie":

What you do to the environment or to other beings in the environment brings similar effects back to you in your life.

Often recognized as the Golden Rule or the Law of Karma, this rule tops the list because it reminds all spiritual practitioners of potential unwanted "rebound" or side effects. As your spiritual power, focus, and abilities grow, this rule will have an ever-greater impact on your life unless you exercise caution. The Universe responds more strongly and powerfully to those with focus, power, and ability.

Note: As humanity moves further in the Aquarian Age, many spiritual practitioners have seen more effects from this rule occur faster. In the past, effects of this rule that often took lifetimes to manifest now occur in minutes, days, weeks, or months. In this particular time in Earth's history, karma seems to operate under a "pay as you go" system. Simply stated, expect the effects of the Law of Karma to occur quickly.

Second Rule: The Judgment of "Good and Bad" According to the Universe
This second rule adds clarity and detail to the first rule described previously:

If you are unsure whether your acts are "good or bad"-- that is, whether those acts are in keeping with universal laws on this planet—the Universe will reflect its judgment back to you quickly, according to the "pay as you go" Law of Karma.

This law holds as true for individuals as it does for entire communities, states, nations, or other organized groups. If you are still unsure of the feedback you receive from the Universe, check areas such as your level of health, the soundness of social relationships, your prosperity or lack of, sufficiency of various needs in life, and even your "luck" with appliances and machines. If your luck appears to be consistently poor, then you are probably acting contrary to universal governing laws, regardless of your intentions. The Universe cares about what you do more than what you intend.

Additional Detailed Rules

The following rules offer more detailed standards by which to measure your acts or the acts of others to determine whether these acts are in accordance with universal laws.

- Do nothing that will harm another being unless you are willing to suffer similar or greater harm. What the Universe considers "harm" may be different than what you consider harm.
- Do not bind another being unless you are willing to be similarly bound. An example of binding someone is doing magickal acts in attempt to coerce a specific other person to act a certain way. There is no problem with attracting desired outcomes into your life, but doing acts that attempt to coerce a specific other person to act in a certain way is a type of binding.
- Never use your spiritual abilities in vain, to show off, or to boost your pride. Using your spiritual abilities from a place of pride usually causes the Universe to bring instant backlash into your life.
- If you choose to charge money or barter for using your spiritual abilities in the service of others, avoid charging extremely high prices. Charge prices for using methods comparable to other professionals, such as an attorney or accountant.
- Never use any spiritual word, chant, litany, or similar "device" unless you are confident in your understanding of its methods, intents, and effects.
- When undertaking a major spiritual operation—one that will require significant effort or attempts to create a major effect in the world—use divination to determine whether you can safely benefit from such

an operation, and to discover the obstacles you must overcome. Divination methods such as pendulum readings, channeling, meditation, and question circles (to name a few) can reveal hidden factors of which you may be unaware.

- In any spiritual endeavor, take your time, think it through, and do it right!

The good news is that you can still use healing magick to heal yourself and your life. The healing rituals we teach in this book won't get you in trouble with the Universe. Instead, you will have a magickal healing toolbox that you can use on yourself and your loved ones with delightful results!

The Ingredients of Healing Magick

"Healing doesn't mean the damage never existed. It means the damage no longer controls your life."
~Akshay Dubey

Many illnesses come from not being able to let go of some issue, hurt or situation. Energy healing and other magickal techniques can help release the emotions created by these instances and healing is then able to occur. Energy healing uses various techniques that enable one to bring disharmonious energy states back into natural balance. Disharmonious energy causes illness, pain and disease because the being that is ill has shifted into an energy state that is not a match for their natural vibrational state. By bringing the vibrational state back into balance, healing occurs. Since we are constantly learning and evolving and the illnesses and diseases we encounter also shift and evolve, healers must keep up with these changes by learning and growing through expansion of their understanding and sensitivity. Some forms of energy healing work on the physical body and others focus more on the energy bodies. Examples of energy healing techniques include using flower essences, aromatherapy, herbs, color, sound, reiki, balancing four-element energies, and Kundalini yoga, to name a few.

If this field of study is of particular interest to you, our ebook, ***Energy Healing for Self and Others***, offers an in-depth study of many of these techniques. The following recipes give more general magickal techniques that can be used in physical, mental, and spiritual healing, and in keeping with the Kitchen Table theme, they are simpler and can be done using ingredients you probably already have at home or can easily get. These recipes have techniques that can be done in conjunction with Western or Eastern medicine remedies and treatments and should not be used solely to the exclusion of advice from your medical practitioner.

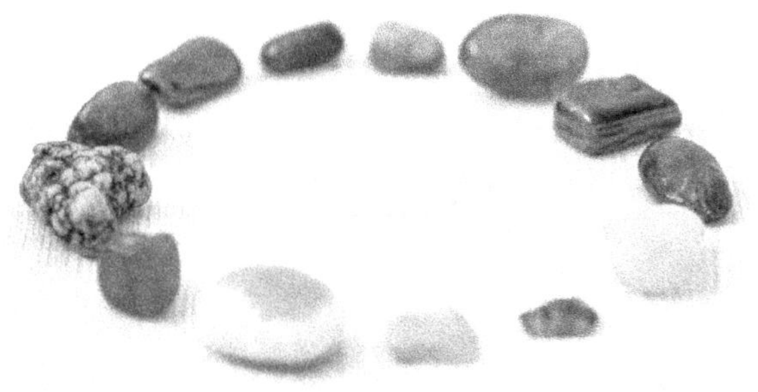

Healing Magick Appetizer Recipes

Appetizers: The Healing Power of Circles

Question Circle

Disconnect Litany

"I feel as if I have finally 'found my voice' after doing the Disconnect Litany in a voice of command. My ex was bothering me on all the time… showing up at my house, at my work, and even during a lunch meeting with a client! Talk about embarrassing. When conventional methods didn't stop him, I asked my friend (who had practiced magick for years) for help. She shared the 'Disconnect Litany' with me, and my life changed forever. I had to repeat the litany several times a week for a few weeks, but eventually my very persistent ex finally left me alone. I finally felt heard and protected. I also felt that the litany helped me heal so that I was ready to look for new and healthier relationships."
~ Bonnie A., Cullman, AL

[this page intentionally left blank]

Question Circle

"Some people see scars, and it is wounding they remember. To me they are proof of the fact that there is healing."
~ Linda Hogan

Time Required: Sixty Minutes

This recipe gives you a way to get guidance and help from the guardians of the four cardinal directions (East, South, West, and North) by using a Question Circle. A Question Circle is an easy way to contact and communicate with the beings of the four directions to get multiple perspectives on a problem or issue in your life. So, in this instance you will be asking for insights on what is causing a specific health issue, whether of a physical, mental or spiritual nature. You may learn where the illness stems from, techniques that would be helpful in releasing the energy that is forming it, spirit guides or totems that can help facilitate healing. Be open to any light these spirit beings can shed on your situation.

Ingredients

- A Sun Yellow (bright yellow with no hints of red or orange) candle
- Wooden or paper matches (no lighters)
- A compass to help locate cardinal directions (North, South, East, West)
- A pen and a pad of paper
- Enough space for a five to 10-foot diameter circle

Recipe Directions

1. Gather your Sun Yellow candle, and a pen and pad of paper for writing.

2. Locate the cardinal directions North, South, East and West.

3. Envision a circle in an open space of about five to 10 feet in diameter.

4. Sit in the South facing North with your Sun Candle in front of you.

5. Light the candle with wooden matches and hold your hands above and around the flame saying:

"Child of wonder,
Child of flame,
Nourish my spirit,
And protect my aim."

6. Sit in the center of the circle facing East, and write your question such as, "What's at the root of this illness?" or "What are the factors surrounding this

disease that I need to know?" or "How can I best heal this illness?"

7. Continue sitting for 3 to 5 minutes just contemplating the question, letting it sit in your mind without trying to answer it.

8. Carry the Sun Yellow candle to the East perimeter of the circle, set the candle down in front of you, and ask your question aloud to the East. Be prepared for a flurry of information. The information usually comes faster than you can write it. You may want to start a new page each time you change directions and label at the top of the page which direction you are addressing. Information may come as images, words you see in your mind or hear in your mind, thoughts or ideas that come to you, or many other ways. Be open to receiving them all.

9. Write the information you receive down on your paper until the flow of information stops and then send your thanks out in that direction.

10. Move in a clockwise fashion to the next direction—the South—and repeat the process.

11. Go all the way around the circle, moving clockwise when changing to a new direction and do the same process with each of the directions. You address the East, then the South, then the West, and finally the North.

12. Once you have addressed all the directions in this manner, come and sit back in the center of the circle facing East again.

13. Send your thanks out all the way around the circle and blow out your Sun Candle.

How to Use the Results of Your Recipe

Sit and read the information you wrote that was received from each direction. Each direction will give you different types of information. For instance, the East will give you information about communication, planning, and ideas. The South will give you guidance on action steps, will power, energy, and desire. The West will give you feelings and spirit guidance, while the North will give you practical steps to take.

Disconnect Litany

"You have the power to heal your life, and you need to know that. We think so often that we are helpless, but we're not. We always have the power of our minds...Claim and consciously use your power."
~ Louise L. Hay

Time Required: Sixty Minutes

If you have something in your life that is really bothering you or stressing you out, you can use the simple magickal litany in this recipe to "cut the cord" from that problem. This could lead to not only peace and healing of mind and your mental state, but also any physical illness that may be manifesting as a result. In some instances, in the case of chronic conditions, we start identifying with the condition and that makes it hard to let go of. For example, one client I knew with migraines of course did not want to live with this pain, but part of her identified who she was as a woman with migraines. This part of her had trouble with letting the migraines go because who would she be without her migraines? Doing this disconnect litany is a great way to deal with these hard to let go issues.

Ingredients

- A Sun Yellow (bright yellow with no hints of red or orange) candle
- Wooden or paper matches (no lighters)
- A compass to help locate cardinal directions (North, South, East, West)
- A pen and a pad of paper
- A dry sage stick (so it burns easily)
- A plate or bowl to catch the ashes as the sage stick burns
- Enough space for a five to 10-foot diameter circle
- A printed version of the following disconnect litany:

"I am neither your creature nor your get,
To be ruled by your whim or your let,
I will go my own way by night or by day,
To serve my own purposes yet!"

Recipe Directions

1. Using your compass outdoors (compasses do not work accurately indoors), locate the four directions of East, South, West, and North.

2. Move back inside your house and clear an area at least 5 to 10 feet in diameter. Mark the four cardinal directions, either in your mind or with sticky notes on the floor.

3. Gather all your materials and sit in the South facing North, with your materials in front of you.

4. Light the candle with the wooden or paper matches. Wait until the candle has a tall working flame. Then

cup your hands over and around the flame and say
aloud in a voice of command:

5. Wait a few moments for the energy of the charge verse
    to fill the space.

6. Light your sage stick from the yellow candle. Once the
    sage stick is burning, stand up, carrying the burning
    sage stick over your plate or bowl to catch the ashes.
    Walk in a clockwise direction around the circle. Allow
    the sage smoke to create a "perimeter" around the
    circle. Once you have walked completely around the
    circle and are back in the South, move to the center of
    the circle.

7. Place your burning sage stick in the bowl or plate.
    Bring the rest of your materials and situate yourself so
    you are facing East with your materials in front of you.

8. Looking outside the circle to the East, "mock up" the
    person or thing from which you want to disconnect. In
    the case of illness or pain, it may be your symptoms or
    the pain itself that you wish to disconnect from. If you
    are needing to disconnect from another person who
    keeps bringing you back into an unhealthy
    relationship, mock up that person standing outside
    the circle. If you want to disconnect from compulsive
    thoughts, see those thoughts written in neon hanging
    in the air outside your circle. If you want to break
    from an unhealthy habit, mock up a version of
    yourself outside the circle in the act of the unhealthy
    habit.

9. Once you have a clear and strong mock up, say the
   following litany in a voice of command:

10. As you say the litany, see the mocked-up energy forms
    outside your circle shrinking and disappearing in a
    puff of smoke. You may have to repeat the disconnect
    litany several times before you achieve the full effect.

11. Once you are done, walk around your circle clockwise
    once more and see if you notice a difference in the
    energy.

12. During your day, if you feel the reappearance of
    whatever you disconnected from, repeat the
    disconnect litany. You can sit inside your car and see
    the mock up outside your car. Repeat the litany three
    times.

13. When you have time, repeat the full procedure with
    the candle and sage stick. Repeat as many times as
    needed. You will be surprised to notice the change in
    your life if you are persistent in using the litany.

How to Use the Results of Your Recipe

The disconnect litany is a wonderful and simple
magickal solution to distance yourself from problems and
issues that are particularly chronic in your life. These types
of chronic problems cause not only mental and spiritual
distress, but can also manifest as various illnesses and
diseases. Whether you are dealing with a sticky and
unhealthy relationship that keeps pulling you in like the tar
baby or have difficulty letting go of some compulsive
thoughts, this recipe can help you untangle yourself from the

problem. After you clear the issue, because you have free will, you can find yourself starting to engage in the same type of thoughts or behaviors that led to your illness or problem, but if you will observe this, catch yourself, and put your attention elsewhere, you can stay disconnected from the problem. If you do not catch yourself and find you have let it take over again, simply do another disconnect litany.

[this page intentionally left blank]

Healing Magick Main Course Recipes

Main Courses: Getting "Hands-On" with the Four Elements

Unwinding the Unwanted Using the Pendulum

Four-Element Healing

Electric Blue Spiral

"I have really enjoyed using these simple healing rituals because I can do them quickly to heal any 'dis-ease' I might experience. I use one of these rituals almost daily and I highly recommend them to anyone who wants to be able to heal themselves energetically."
~ Katherine G., Medford, OR.

[this page intentionally left blank]

Unwinding the Unwanted Using the Pendulum

"Healing requires from us not to stop struggling, but to enjoy life more and endure it less."
~ Darina Stoyanova

Time Required: Sixty Minutes

This recipe can help you resolve issues that are causing illness or disease once you have identified them. If you are not aware of the emotions, thoughts, or issues that are causing your illness or disease, then you may need to do the Question Circle as described in a previous recipe first. Once you know what you need to release in order to facilitate healing, you can literally unwind your problems with this simple pendulum recipe. You can use the pendulum each day to spin away health problem as needed; sometimes a health problem will mutate or lead to some other issue may need healing.

Ingredients

- A pendulum. You can either purchase one, or make one yourself using a string or chain plus a small object such as a stone or paperclip.
- An indicator plate made from paper circle with "Yes" written to the left of the center of the paper and "No" written to the right of the center of the paper (see the following diagram).
- An understanding of the emotions, thoughts, or issue that is contributing to your mental, spiritual, or physical illness or disease.

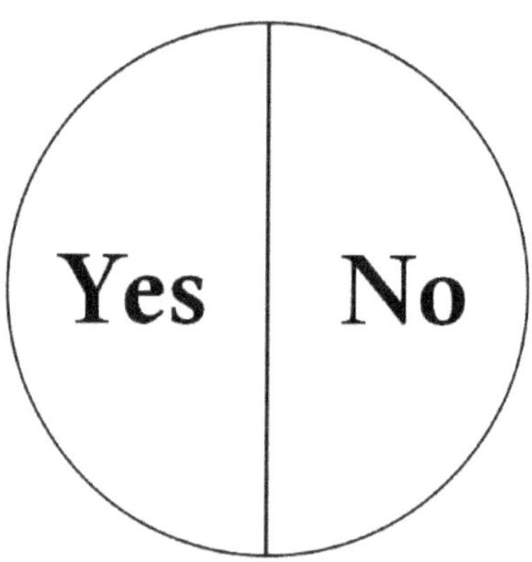

Sample Indicator Plate

Recipe Directions

1. Hold your pendulum in your dominant hand (the hand with which you naturally point), letting the pendulum dangle while you visualize the problem you wish to clear.

2. Ask your pendulum, "Can I and may I clear this situation?" If you get a 'Yes' answer from your pendulum, then proceed to the next step. You may use an indicator plate (see the previous diagram) to get this answer. As you hold the pendulum over the center of the paper let it spin. When it stops spinning over

the indicator plate it will swing back and forth. One side of the swing will be longer than the other. The side that has the longer swing will be your answer. Should your pendulum indicate, "No," do not proceed. Instead, reframe the question and ask your pendulum again. For instance, if you received a "No" to the question, "Can I and may I clear the situation causing my ankle pain?", reframe the question. You might instead ask, "Can I and may I clear the situation causing physical pain in my body?" If your pendulum consistently gives you "No" answers, do not proceed. Instead go back to the previous section on "Question Circles" to gain a more definitive understanding of the causes of your health problems. Then return to the first step of this ritual and ask a more refined question based on your new understanding.

3. After receiving a "Yes" from the pendulum, you may proceed with the "unwinding" process. Begin swinging your pendulum in a counter clockwise direction, asking your pendulum to clear the situation. As you do this, "see" the situation resolving in your mind. Be very specific with your request, and how you envision as to the situation being resolved. Focus on what your life would look like if the situation disappeared from your life, but do not focus on how you think it should be resolved. Do not think about the steps you think should be taken for resolution. The Universe is in charge of the actual steps; your job is merely to focus on the intended result.

4. Continue to focus on clearing the situation until your pendulum stops spinning in the counter clockwise direction. It will then either start moving along a vertical or horizontal axis, stop spinning completely, or start spinning clockwise. When your pendulum stops swinging on its own then the problem has been cleared.

How to Use the Results of Your Recipe

This ritual is also a good, quick way to clear up problems or snags that come up in your day. Once a problem has been cleared you can, of course, always choose to bring it back simply by the power of your negative thoughts or focus. Trust the power of your pendulum and your intent and release the problem from your consciousness. If you find it seeping back into your consciousness throughout the day, change your focus to something else.

You can use a variation of this technique to diagnose and treat others. Have the other person lie down, spin your pendulum in a clockwise direction starting at their head. State your intention and focus, that you want to find areas that need healing or are a source of pain. Continue to let the pendulum spin in a clockwise direction as you slowly move it down over the person's body. Note the places where your pendulum stops spinning, changes direction, or begins to swing in a straight line. These spots are the places that need healing. Now swing the pendulum in a counter-clockwise direction over each problem area that your pendulum identified, holding your intention and focus on healing the area. Continue letting the pendulum swing over the area until it stops spinning counter-clockwise, which indicates that the problem has been cleared.

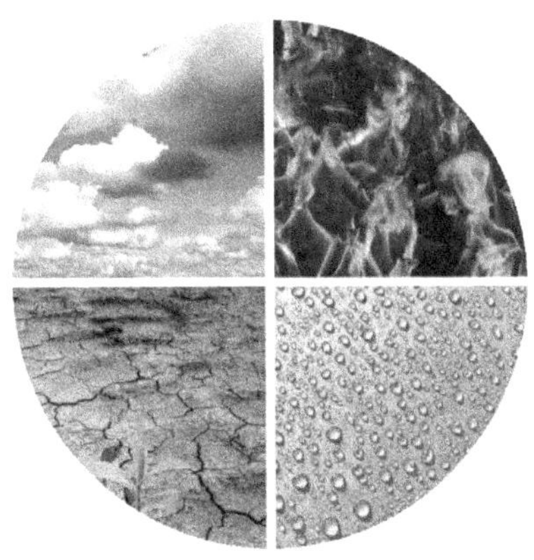

Four-Element Healing

"Every breath and every step can be nourishing and healing."
~ Thich Nhat Hanh

Time Required: Fifteen Minutes

At the foundation of all magickal studies is an understanding of the four elements: Air, Fire, Water and Earth. One of the basic tenets of magickal studies is that everything in this Universe is made up of some combination of these four elements, and if you understand and know how to work with these elements, you can understand (and create) anything you desire. In the case of healing, your body can be responding to an excess of a certain type of elemental energy or a lack of it. This recipe gives you a technique in which to use each element to take on more of a particular element or to reduce the amount of that element you have.

Ingredients

- Read through the following "Recipe Directions" and gather the ingredients for the portions of the rituals that apply to your situation. There are specific recipes for each of the four magickal elements (Air, Fire, Water, and Earth). These recipes can be used to increase, decrease, or change the type of energy from your physical or energetic bodies.

Recipe Directions

In this section you will find specific recipes for each of the four magickal elements (Air, Fire, Water, and Earth). These recipes can be used to increase, decrease, or change the type of energy from your physical or energetic bodies.

AIR: Air Boxes

An Air box is an energetic box filled with an Air color and possibly an Air characteristic, created by the aura energy of your hands. When your hands are relaxed, the aura energies around them are relatively small and close to the skin. When you move your hands, you send energy down into them and the aura expands or "flares." You create boxes with these energies as a safe, controlled, and effective way to add or subtract air colors and/or characteristics from your overall energy balances. When you have a shortage of a particular type of Air energy, you can take on a box to increase that energy in yourself. When you have too much of that type energy, you can dump a box of it. Excesses or shortages of the Air element can cause various illnesses, disturbances, issues or conditions.

Ingredients for Air Boxes

- A color source for clear, white, and/or sky blue
- The energy from your own hands.
- A square mailing box (optional, and only necessary if you need to practice the hand movements to form an Air box shape).

Air Box Recipe Directions

1. Have a clear, white, and/or sky blue color source available before you start building your box. As you form your box, make the following hand motions in a smooth, unbroken pattern.

    - Form the top and bottom of the box by placing your hands, palms facing each other as if holding a box between them with hands on top and bottom of the box. Start with your hands farther apart and bring them together, "pressing" the energy together.
    - Form the front and back of the box, moving your hands again with palms facing in a position as if you were holding a box on its front and back sides. Press the energy together in this position.
    - Use your hands now in the same way to form the left and right sides of the box.
    - Leave your hands in this last position, as it will hold together as long as you hold the sides of the box.

2. Decide which color with which you want to fill your Air box. A magickal Air box must be filled with an Air color. Air energy colors are:

    - Clear: This color is associated with physical air, and is associated with breathing, physical reactions, physical sensations, and seeing,
    - White: This color is associated with the mental aspect of the magickal element Air, such any mental processes, thinking, planning, and communicating.
    - Sky Blue: This color is associated with Spirit, including spiritual enlightenment, wisdom, and understanding.

3. If you have determined that you need more of a

particular for healing, you can do so by filling the box with your chosen Air color. For instance, if you are having trouble breathing due to a respiratory illness, you can improve your breathing by filling an Air box with clear Air. Or if you want to improve your mental acuity before taking a test, build an Air box filled with white Air energy. Fill the box by holding the box in front of your eyes and in line with the color source, pulling the color into the box with your intention and "energetic pull." Keep filling the Air box until it is full. Do not think about this step, just do it. Your intention will do the work of filling the box. You will know that your box is full when your hands grow warm or tingly (this takes about five to 15 seconds). You can't overfill a box so don't worry about doing so. A magickal Air box will only accept a certain amount of energy.

4. Once you have created and filled your Air box, take it on by bringing it towards your face. At the same time, "snort" or breathe in the box.

5. In addition to increasing your Air energies by breathing in Air boxes, you can also decrease your Air energies by dumping Air boxes. To dump Air energy, build an empty box as explained previously. Now look at your color source, and breathe (or blow) the color out of your body and into the box until the box is full. Dump the box by throwing it into any upper corner of a room, or by breaking it on your knee. Be careful not to throw your Air box at a person or animal accidentally, since you don't know the consequences that might occur.

How to Use the Results of Your Air Box Recipe

If you don't feel any noticeable difference after 15 minutes, increase or decrease your Air energies by taking on or off another of the same box. Do the same with a third box if necessary. Sometimes, our natural balances make it difficult to feel the result of certain boxes. For example, if you are very deficient in a certain energy, it may take a while to feel the difference.

Fire: Hugging Your Fridge

Your refrigerator is a great magick tool because it is an electrical ground or conduit. That means it can ground out excess Fire energies that are either physical or psychic. Pain, stress, anger, inflammation, fever, headache, and anxiety are all mostly Fire energies. When you have these symptoms, you have an excess of some type of Fire energy. You can use your refrigerator as a magickal tool to ground out the excess energy.

Ingredients for Hugging Your Fridge
- A refrigerator or other large, grounded appliance
- A Sun Yellow candle (with no orange or red tones)
- Paper or wooden matches
- A red-orange color source (the same color as road hazard signs)

Recipe Directions for Hugging Your Fridge
1. If you can place the area of your body containing the pain, stress, or inflammation directly on the fridge, then do so. For example, if you have a headache at the front of your head, place your forehead against the refrigerator. If the headache is in the back of your head, then put the back of your head against the refrigerator. If you are dealing with overall aches or stress, lie down on the floor and put your feet on the refrigerator.

2. Focus your attention on the symptom you want to eliminate, such as pain or inflammation. Start flowing that energy into the refrigerator, using your fridge as a magickal grounding tool. Fire energy flows quickly so you will only need to flow for a minute or two. Feel yourself pushing the symptom out of your body and,

letting it flow into the fridge.

3. Once you have finished flowing out the excess Fire
    energy safely into the refrigerator, light a Sun Yellow
    candle with paper or wooden matches. Put your hands
    over the flame (not so close that you get burned
    though), and pull Sun Yellow energy into your body.
    Sun Yellow is a healing form Fire energy. This
    replaces the Fire energy you put in the fridge so that
    you are not deficient in Fire energy after hugging your
    fridge. A minute or two of pulling in this healing
    energy in should be long enough to restore your Fire
    energies.

How to Use the Results of the "Hugging Your Fridge" Recipe

This technique of using your refrigerator as a
magickal tool works well for reducing almost any kind of
pain or inflammation, including stress, anger, fever,
headache, and anxiety. If you find the pain getting worse
after doing this procedure, you are possibly dealing with a
buried unconscious issue, which must be handled in a totally
different way. This is rare, but if it happens, take some
Rescue Remedy (a flower essence mixture available in most
health food stores) and stop flowing energy. This will prevent
the buried unconscious issue from causing problems in
present time. You will need to seek out a qualified esoteric
healer to help you handle these types of issues.

Water: Shower Litany –

Find yourself in pain or stressed out at the end of the
day? If so, then here's a recipe for you! You can literally wash
tension, strain and pain off your body in the shower or
bathtub using the shower litany.

Ingredients for Shower Litany

*   Access to a shower or other type of cool running water
    that is tall enough that you can easily stand under it

- Alternately you can use a tub of cool water from which you can easily drain water

Recipe Directions for Shower Litany

1. Run water in your shower until the water temperature is cool (just below body temperature). Water that is too cold creates tension, while water that is too hot will not carry fire energy away.

2. Get in the shower with your back to the showerhead.

3. Move the showerhead so that the water is hitting you at the base of the skull and the water is able to run evenly over your back and front.

4. Stand this way in the stream of water and feel the tension or pain or other Fire type energy moving down your body being absorbed by the water.

5. If you need to you can run your hands down your body to bring the tension and pain down to your feet.

6. Picture and "feel" the tension and pain mixing with the water and flowing down the drain, while simultaneously repeating the following litany aloud in a voice with authority and power.

> *"All the tension, all the strain,*
> *All the pain with excess flame,*
> *Flow with water, down the drain!"*

7. Keep saying the litany until you feel all the tension and pain leave your body.

How to Use the Results of Your Shower Litany Recipe

The shower litany will wash away any inflammation, pain, headache, tension, or stress that you have accumulated during the day. Using it daily will help you avoid picking up Fire energies such as stress, pain and anxiety throughout your day. Used daily, it can also help you feel more balanced and more energetic. Use reminders with laminated sticky notes that have the verse printed on them in your bathroom or in the shower so you don't forget to use this recipe as a daily ritual.

You can also do this ritual in a bathtub filled with cool water by seeing the Fire energies flowing out of your body, being absorbed by the water and then draining the water from the tub and watching them flow down the drain. Say the litany in the same way as for the shower litany, remaining in the tub until all the water drains out, taking the Fire energies with it.

Earth: Rooting

Rooting is a great way to ground out Fire energies such as pain, anger, frustration, stress, and use Earth energies to regain balance – physical, mental, and spiritual. Rooting allows you to develop "roots" from your palms, heels or base of your spine. You can then plant them into the Earth to get rid of unwanted energies and to receive healing energies directly from the Earth itself. Use rooting to balance your energy or mood swings, stay focused in present time and dump negative energy.

Ingredients for Rooting
- A comfortable place to sit on a chair or on the floor
- Several minutes of quiet time and space

Recipe Directions
1. Place your heels, palms or seat (or all three) on the ground. You can extend roots from more than one body part at once.

2. Envision yourself forming roots from your palms, heels. or the base of your spine. Begin extending those roots with your intention. You don't need to think

about it, just do it! Some people find it easier to do this process with eyes closed.

3. Push your roots through the carpet or tile, into the sub-floor and down into the Earth. If you are in a multi-level building, you will need to go through each level until you reach the Earth. If you are wearing shoes with thick soles, you may have to extend the roots out the sides of your shoes.

4. Once your roots reach the Earth, keep extending them down through the topsoil and deeper layers until you reach bedrock.

5. When you reach bedrock, lock your roots in.

6. Sit quietly with your roots in the Earth, and just breathe naturally.

7. With each exhale, send any unwanted energies, illness, pain, or negative emotions down your roots into the bedrock. The Earth is highly receptive, and will receive these energies easily.

8. With each inhale pull in minerals, fluids, and other energies from the Earth for nourishment and balancing. You don't have to specify what you're pulling up – your body and your roots will work automatically with the Earth to pull up what is needed.

9. Once you feel relaxed and nourished. pull your roots back up into your body. Stay seated until you have totally pulled your "roots" back in.

How to Use the Results of Your Rooting Recipe
Always be sure to pull your roots back in completely. If you stand up without doing so, you may feel a slight

"popping" sensation and your body will be sore for a few days. Rooting can help you feel refreshed, awake, alive and balanced. This recipe only takes a few minutes and is worth every second! You can use this recipe when you are alone or in public and no one will know what you are doing.

Electric Blue Spiral

"Healing doesn't eliminate all the hard moments. It changes how you handle them."
~ Thema Bryant-Davis

Time Required: Thirty Minutes

Electric blue is a very powerful Fire element energy. It is the energy that forms galaxies, is the creator of the Four Elements, and is also the energy associated with most psychic vibrations. It is the same color that is at the base of a gas flame, very bright and very intense. If you have trouble controlling your magickal abilities in certain situations, you can focus on electric blue energy to stay in control. It is often used for creating protection shields around yourself or property and in other magickal self-defense type techniques.

Ingredients
- Electric blue color source
- A comfortable place to sit

- Ten to fifteen minutes of quiet uninterrupted time

Recipe Directions

1. Envision an electric blue spiral spinning inside your chest, near your heart chakra.

2. If you were to "look down" at the blue spiral, you want to see it spinning clockwise.

3. Some people see a laser-like spiral while others see more of an amorphous flame. The goal is to focus all of your magickal energy into that spiral.

4. When you focus on the spiral, your attention (and your energy) is fully contained within yourself. You are shielded, both from projecting your energy outward and from absorbing unwanted energies from other people.

5. See the electric blue spiral inside yourself attacking your health problem, illness or disease, and/or burning up whatever toxins or harmful substances are in your body.

6. You can do this for a short amount of time and then see the spiral stopping movement and dissipating or you can go for a longer time, keeping the spiral with you throughout the day.

How to Use the Results of Your Recipe

You can experiment with using the electric blue spiral in a clockwise rotation and a counter-clockwise rotation to decide which way feels best to you. It may be that with certain conditions it will seem best one direction, and with others it will seem best the opposite direction. With practice you can use this technique while you go about your day doing other things. It is also a very powerful technique to do in the "in between" period before you fall asleep and just as you start to wake up. This "twilight" time of consciousness can magnify the power of any magickal rituals you perform.

[this page intentionally left blank]

Healing Magick Dessert Recipes
Desserts: Sweet Healing Magick Rituals

Healing Exit Ritual

Moving Energy to Clear Blockages

"When I was going through a really rough patch in my life, both physically and emotionally, I found real solace and healing in the simple "healing grace" exit ritual. It helped me to see my blessings every day, rather than fret about my worries and troubles."
~ Yolanda Y., Tampa, FL

[this page intentionally left blank]

Healing Exit Ritual

"I go to nature to be soothed, healed and have my senses put in order."
~ John Burroughs

The Exit Ritual is one of three parts of the Navajo Beauty Way. It is a contact and greeting ritual that connects you with higher powers and beings and is totally non-denominational so it doesn't matter what Higher Power you believe in or what, if any, religious practices you adhere to. It can also be used to realign our chi or life force, which can become distorted from working and living in buildings with strong electromagnetic fields and thus increase our energy levels. By using the verbal form presented in this recipe, you will be asking for help from higher beings in dealing with your pain, illness or disease.

Ingredients
- The willingness to use this recipe every time you step outside
- The openness to connecting with spiritual beings and accepting their help

Recipe Directions

1. Every time you leave an enclosed space (i.e., your home, a building of any kind, a car, and other similar places), look up towards the sky once you are outside, extend your focus and out loud say, "Sky Above."

2. Keep focusing awareness above you and now extend your focus into the Earth and say out loud, "And Earth Below."

3. Keep awareness focused now both above and below, say out loud, "Embracing Your Healing Grace, I Greet You."

4. Pause for a few moments longer and be aware of either some kind of change within yourself (change of attitude, new awareness), a change in the environment (sudden breeze, change in color of sky, animal or bird suddenly appearing, plant life becoming vividly visible), or a message from Sky or Earth heard like a voice in your head (answer to question, new direction, guidance).

5. You can also raise arms in a V toward Sky for step one and lower them in a V towards the Earth for step two.

How to Use the Results of Your Recipe

The Exit Ritual can bring you a sense of peace and serenity. It can also help you establish relationships with higher beings who can help you gain information or work on manifestations. Deep inside, you are always peaceful, happy and serene - sometimes you just don't know how to access that part of yourself. So, if you find yourself getting frustrated, negative or stressed out, go outside and do the Exit Ritual.

If you are in a public place with a lot of people around you may initially feel that doing this makes you uncomfortable. That's OK, you don't have to use the arm motions. If you find this embarrassment factor coming into play you also don't have to say the words too loud, but you do need to vocalize them. You'll probably find with time that most people won't really notice what you are doing (they're more concerned with their own happenings) and that it will look to them like you are just standing still for a brief time trying to remember something.

[this page intentionally left blank]

Moving Energy to Clear Blockages

"The pain of yesterday is the strength of today."
~ Paulo Coelho

Time Required: Thirty Minutes

Sometimes physical pain and discomfort is the result of stuck or stagnant energy in the body. Our energy can get stuck because of a sedentary lifestyle, old injuries, stress, resentments...the list goes on. In short, we can have stuck energy as a result of everyday events and situations, which results in physical pain. This recipe gives you an easy way to clear energy blockages and get your energy moving freely again, thus leading to healing.

Ingredients
- A comfortable place to sit
- 10 to 20 minutes of quiet, uninterrupted time
-

Recipe Directions

1. Sit in a comfortable position and close your eyes.

2. Relax and breathe for a few moments.

3. Begin by noticing feelings or sensations in your left hand. Some people experience a feeling of warmth or tingling. The sensation may be different for you. It doesn't matter so long as you are aware of sensation in your left hand.

4. Gently move that sensation up your left arm, across your back, down your right arm, and onto your right hand.

5. Now reverse the movement and move the sensation along the same path from your right hand back to your left hand.

6. Now put the sensation on your left foot, and move it up your left leg, across your waist, down your right leg and onto your right foot.

7. Now reverse the movement and move the sensation along the same path from your right leg back to your left leg.

8. Finally, put the sensation at the base of your spine and move that sensation slowly up your spine to the top of your head.

9. Keeping that sensation there, say aloud, "I am."

10. Release your attention from the sensation at the top of your head. Relax and breathe deeply for a few minutes. Open your eyes.

How to Use the Results of Your Recipe

Doing this healing magick ritual on a regular basis will keep your body free of most energy blockages, and will have a calm, soothing effect on your spirit. The best way to heal illness and disease is to prevent them from occurring in the first place. This recipe, done on a regular basis, keeps your energy flows moving and clear of blockages that can cause pain and illness.

[this page intentionally left blank]

More Magickal Resources

Kindle or Paperback on Amazon:
1. ***Witchcraft Spell Book Series:***
   - Learn How to Do Witchcraft Rituals and Spells with Your Bare Hands (Witchcraft Spell Books, Book 1)
   - Learn How to Do Witchcraft Rituals and Spells with Household Ingredients (Witchcraft Spell Books, Book 2)
   - Learn How to Do Witchcraft Rituals and Spells with Magical Tools (Witchcraft Spell Books, Book 3)
   - Witchcraft Spell Book: The Complete Guide of Witchcraft Rituals & Spells for Beginners (compilation of Books 1, 2 & 3)
2. ***Kitchen Table Magick Series***

Ebooks and Online Courses at *www.shamanschool.com*
   - Wand: Air Tool
   - Athame: Fire Tool
   - Chalice: Water Tool
   - Plate: Earth Tool
   - Magical Tool: Firebowl
   - Psychic Development
   - Energy Healing For Self and Others

-
- How to Do Voodoo
- Daily Rituals to Attract What You Want in Life

Find a complete list of magickal resources on https://amzn.to/3swxvPo. These resources are constantly updated so check back often!

Free Gift Offer

To thank you for purchasing this book, I'd like to give you a

100% FREE GIFT

Learn more about your free magickal gift.

Access Your Free Gift at *www.shamanschool.com*

Find a complete list of magickal resources on https://amzn.to/3swxvPo. These resources are constantly updated so check back often!

About G. Alan Joel

Magick means many things to different people. The form of magick taught by G. Alan Joel for more than 30 years is steeped in tribal traditions from around the world, from both modern tribal cultures and those from the past, which have been mostly passed on through oral dialog.

At the very heart of the magick that Mr. Joel teaches is the use of Universal Laws for the benefit of self, others, and even the planet. These magickal traditions can take on many forms, including simple rituals for daily use, specific spells for particular life situations, the use of simulacra (often better known as voodoo), weather working, water witching, the use of the elemental tools (Firebowl, Wand, Athame, Chalice, and Plate), magickal self-defense rituals, and more. Also included are the use of the Tarot for divination and spellwork, divination rituals of all kinds, Spirit-to-Spirit communication, exercises for psychic development, and abundant healing techniques.

Through his 30 plus years of studying, teaching, and honing his magickal practice, G. Alan Joel has helped thousands of people successfully integrate the magickal, and seemingly miraculous, into their daily lives. In fact, one of the greatest gifts Mr. Joel has offered through his teachings is the ability for his students to always find a magickal solution for life situations that often seem impossible to solve. With magick, anything is possible in the mundane world. All that is required of the practitioner is an open mind, the desire to learn, and a willingness to pay some time and effort into his or her magickal practice. One of Mr. Joel's favorite quotes is:

"What you pay into your practice pays you back!"

While many magickal traditions have fiercely guarded their secrets from the public, Mr. Joel feels that "Magick is the birthright of every planetary citizen." As such he strives to offer magickal teachings that are easily learned and inexpensive (no excessive fees to join exclusive magickal groups or ascend up the levels of learning). He also offers techniques that are usable and effective for all who are sincere in their desire to practice magick. In essence, Mr. Joel's methods teach a form of "Every Man's (and Woman's) Magick." All are welcome, his teachings are simple yet effective, and he also offers online classes in which he helps students troubleshoot their magickal issues in an interactive setting.

Find out more about Mr. Joel's teachings here and on his website (***www.shamanschool.com***) where magickal offerings are updated on a regular basis.

Mr. Joel augments this magickal knowledge and teaching with 30 years of practice as Doctor of Chinese Medicine, including a deep understanding of herbology and acupuncture. His understanding of the healing arts deepens the magickal knowledge he teaches, as magickal healing is a major aspect of his teachings. Mr. Joel believes that while there is clearly a time and place for Western Medicine, magickal and Eastern healing techniques can be harmoniously blended in to offer people many choices for healing all types of health conditions.

About the Esoteric School of Shamanism and Magic

The Esoteric School of Shamanism and Magic was started from a desire for all people from all over the globe to be able to attend a real, if virtual, school dedicated to magick and shamanism. The aim of the Esoteric School of Shamanism and Magic is to help people create permanent, positive change in their lives through the study of esoteric magickal and shamanic knowledge. It doesn't matter what your esoteric background is, whether you started out with witchcraft, religious studies, spirituality or candle magick, we welcome you. We believe that the Truth is the same, no matter which form you practice. We delight in all manner of shamanic schools and traditions, magickal techniques and esoteric ritual. You can visit us at **_www.shamanschool.com_**, our blog at **_http://shamanmagic.blogspot.com_**, or on social media via links on our website.

[this page intentionally left blank]

[this page intentionally left blank]

[this page intentionally left blank]

[this page intentionally left blank]